His Heart, Her Fire

His Heart, Her Fire

Balancing Flames of Love in Marriage

B. Vincent

QuillQuest Publishers

CONTENTS

CONTENTS

Chapter 1: Introduction

Setting the Stage: Inside the multifaceted embroidered artwork of marriage, the fragile dance of adoration and understanding is principal. In this initial part, we establish the groundwork for our investigation of conjugal concordance. We dive into the quintessence of adjusting love, remembering it not just as a heartfelt idea but rather as an essential element for the food of a profoundly satisfying organization. Here, we disclose the meaning of supporting the blazes of warmth and sympathy, cultivating a climate where the two accomplices can flourish inwardly, intellectually, and profoundly. Through impactful stories and immortal insight, we welcome you to consider the significant ramifications of developing a fair love inside the hallowed association of marriage. As we leave on this excursion together, let us enlighten the way toward an agreeable and getting through bond that rises above the customary, lighting the flares of energy and figuring out in each heart.

Figuring out the Blazes: In the multifaceted trap of conjugal elements, each accomplice delivers an exceptional mix of characteristics, qualities, and quirks. Here, we set out on a significant excursion of self-disclosure and shared understanding, disentangling the strings of singularity that shape the texture of our association. Through reflection and compassion, we enlighten the nuanced intricacies of one another's hearts, perceiving the assorted tints that make the material out of our common life. With a caring look, we honor the lavishness of our disparities, commending the different viewpoints and encounters that enhance our excursion together. As we dig into the profundities of our spirits, we develop a significant appreciation for the pith of our darling, winding around an embroidery of adoration that distinctions and embraces the sum of what our identity is. In this section, we welcome you to leave on an extraordinary odyssey of mindfulness and sympathy, cultivating a more profound association that rises above the limits of distinction, and supporting the blazes of affection that join us as one.

Planning the Excursion: As we set out on this journey towards conjugal agreement, graphing our course with lucidity and intentionality is fundamental. In this section, we disclose the guide that will direct us through the maze of affection, offering a thorough outline of the landscape we are going to navigate. With accuracy and prescience, we depict the important milestones and waypoints that will intersperse our excursion, from the shores of correspondence to the pinnacles of profound closeness and the valleys of compromise. From the perspective of astuteness and experience, we give knowledge into the difficulties and wins that lie ahead, outfitting you with the devices and techniques expected to explore the intricacies of marriage with effortlessness and strength. With each page turned, we coax you to go along with us on this odyssey of revelation and change, welcoming you to investigate the profundities of your heart and the unlimited capability of your association. Together, let us set out on this sacrosanct journey, directed by the radiance of affection and the commitment of a common fate.

Embracing the Greeting: With hearts open and spirits adjusted, we stretch out a warm greeting to set out on an excursion of significant importance and limitless potential. In this finishing up fragment of our early on part, we coax you to embrace the valuable chance to dive further into the domains of adoration, association, and common figuring out inside your marriage. As we stand at the edge of change, we welcome you to throw away the shadows of uncertainty and dread, and step intensely into the iridescent domain of probability. With steady responsibility and steadfast determination, let us leave on this holy mission together, joined by the normal motivation behind supporting and supporting the flares of affection inside our relationships. As we venture forward, may our hearts be loaded up with trust, our brains with insight, and our spirits with vast love, as we explore the wondrous embroidery of conjugal euphoria.

2

Chapter 2: Understanding Individual Flames

Investigating One of a kind Characteristics: Inside the sacrosanct space of marriage, each accomplice delivers a kaleidoscope of qualities, eccentricities, and interests that paint the material of their common presence. In this section, we leave on an excursion of disclosure, diving into the profundities of distinction to uncover the unlikely treasures that characterize our embodiment. From the perspective of contemplation and interest, we explore the maze of character, disentangling the complicated embroidered artwork of qualities that make us what our identity is. From the calm contemplation of one to the abundant energy of different, we commend the kaleidoscope of characteristics that join us in adoration. With every disclosure, we develop a more profound appreciation for the extraordinary gifts and points of view that each accomplice offers of real value, cultivating a climate of shared regard and deference. As we set out on this journey of self-disclosure and understanding, may we embrace the extravagance of our singular flares, touching off the flash of adoration that will enlighten our way ahead.

Perceiving Qualities and Shortcomings: In the complex dance of marriage, recognizing the range of qualities and shortcomings that shape the texture of our partnership is basic. This part fills in as a reference point of reflection, directing us through the maze of mindfulness to uncover the jewels of our capacities and constraints. With delicate respect, we look at the scene of our assets, recognizing the gifts and abilities that improve our association and move us towards significance. However, with equivalent veneration, we go up against the shadows of our shortcomings, perceiving the regions where development and backing are required. Through this excursion of acknowledgment and acknowledgment, we develop a significant comprehension of ourselves and our accomplices, encouraging a climate of sympathy and compassion. As we explore the recurring patterns of coexistence, may we bridle the force of our assets and explore the weaknesses of our shortcomings with effortlessness, sustaining the powers of profound devotion that join us.

Embracing Contrasts: Inside the sacredness of marriage, variety isn't only endured yet celebrated as a fundamental part of our common process. In this part, we set out on a journey of investigation, exploring the oceans of singularity to find the fortunes concealed inside the profundities of our disparities. With open hearts and psyches, we cast to the side the shackles of congruity and embrace the exceptional points of view, inclinations, and peculiarities that recognize each accomplice. From the delicate recurring pattern of one's personality to the intense strokes of different's interests, we honor the kaleidoscope of variety that advances our association. Through this festival of contrasts, we develop a more profound appreciation for the complex mosaic of our organization, winding around an embroidery of adoration that is pretty much as lively and fluctuated as the shades of the rainbow. As we explore the intricacies of hitched life, may we love the magnificence of our variety, tracking down strength and solidarity in the rich woven artwork of our common encounters.

Developing Mindfulness: At the core of each and every flourishing marriage lies a profound well of mindfulness, from which springs the waters of sympathy, understanding, and development. In this part, we set out on an excursion of contemplation, directed by the radiance of self-revelation to enlighten the secret profundities of our spirits. With delicate interest and enduring mental fortitude, we dig into the openings of our being, stripping back the layers of molding and assumption to uncover the center of our valid selves. Through this course of self-disclosure, we gain knowledge into our necessities, wants, and fears, engaging us to explore the flows of hitched existence with effortlessness and deliberateness. As we develop a more profound comprehension of ourselves, we produce a way towards more noteworthy concordance and association inside our relationship. With each step taken on this excursion of mindfulness, may we embrace the magnificence of our independence and honor the consecrated fire that consumes inside us, touching off the flash of adoration that will enlighten our common way ahead.

3

Chapter 3: Communication: Fueling the Fire

The Meaning of Compelling Correspondence: Inside the unpredictable embroidery of marriage, correspondence fills in as the crucial string that ties hearts, brains, and spirits together. In this section, we dive into the significant meaning of viable correspondence as the foundation of a flourishing organization. Through the specialty of talented discourse, couples have the ability to rise above hindrances, fashion profound associations, and support the flares of adoration that support their association. By improving the skill to offer viewpoints, feelings, and wants with clearness and truthfulness, couples lay the preparation for shared figuring out, trust, and closeness. As we set out on this investigation of correspondence, let us perceive filling the flames of adoration inside our relationships, enlightening the way towards more profound association and persevering through harmony extraordinary potential.

Procedures for Undivided attention and Sympathetic Comprehension: In the ensemble of marriage, the song of genuine association is made out of words expressed as well as of the significant craft of tuning in. In this part, we uncover the extraordinary force of undivided attention and sympathetic comprehension as fundamental parts of viable correspondence. Through the act of undivided attention, accomplices figure out how to quiet the clamor of their own contemplations and drench themselves completely in the account of their adored, adjusting their hearts to the subtleties of feeling and expectation. With sympathy as our directing light, we set out on an excursion of significant comprehension, venturing into the shoes of our accomplices to see the world through their eyes, feel their delights and distresses, and approve their encounters. Through these holy practices, couples develop a profound feeling of association and sympathy, encouraging a climate where love can prosper and closeness can flourish. As we embrace the craft of undivided attention and sympathetic comprehension, let us hold nothing back from the orchestra of our accomplice's spirit, winding around an embroidery of affection that rises above words and resounds with the harmonies of common comprehension and sympathy.

Beating Correspondence Hindrances and Misconceptions: Inside the maze of marriage, correspondence can now and again waver, staggering over the rough territory of error and misconception. In this part, we defy the normal impediments that ruin successful correspondence and proposition procedures for beating them with effortlessness and flexibility. Through the delicate specialty of weakness and boldness, couples explore the slippery waters of contention, changing disunity into a chance for development and more profound association. By developing a feeling of sympathy and compassion, accomplices figure out how to connect the split between their contrasting points of view, settling on some mutual interest in the midst of the tumult of conflict. As we venture together through the valleys of miscommunication, let us embrace the difficulties as venturing stones towards more noteworthy comprehension and solidarity, fashioning a way towards persevering through concordance inside our relationships.

Building Trust and Receptiveness Through Discourse: In the sanctum of marriage, trust and transparency structure the bedrock whereupon persevering through adoration is assembled. In this critical section, we investigate the groundbreaking force of exchange in developing a culture of trust and weakness inside the organization. Through genuine and straightforward correspondence, couples make a sacrosanct space where fears can be shared, dreams can be supported, and hearts can be revealed. By cultivating a culture of shared regard and acknowledgment, accomplices produce profound associations that endure the everyday hardships and difficulty. As we explore the landscape of conjugal correspondence, let us embrace the significant closeness that comes from sharing our most profound insights, touching off the flares of trust and receptiveness that enlighten the way towards enduring affection and satisfaction.

4

Chapter 4: Nurturing Emotional Intimacy

Investigating the Profundities of Close to home Association: Inside the sacrosanct association of marriage, profound closeness fills in as the soul that supports the connection between accomplices. In this section, we leave on an excursion into the profundities of profound association, remembering it as the establishment whereupon persevering through affection is fabricated. Through delicate investigation and genuine contemplation, we disentangle the mind boggling strings of feeling that wind around together the texture of our organization. From the delicate bit of a hand to the quiet trade of knowing looks, we praise the heap manners by which we express and get love in its most perfect structure. As we dive into the maze of close to home closeness, let us embrace the weakness and legitimacy that lie at its center, producing an association that rises above the customary and lights the flares of enthusiasm and commitment inside our souls.

Developing Closeness Through Weakness and Realness: In the safe-haven of marriage, weakness and validness are the sacrosanct keys that open the way to genuine closeness. In this section, we enlighten the extraordinary force of weakness, welcoming accomplices to strip back the layers of misrepresentation and uncover their most valid selves. Through demonstrations of mental fortitude and trust, we make a place of refuge where fears can be shared, instabilities recognized, and dreams sustained. By embracing weakness as a pathway to association, we make ready for more profound comprehension and acknowledgment inside the relationship. As we venture together towards more prominent closeness, let us honor the mental fortitude it takes to be really valid, and praise the significant magnificence of adoration that twists in the rich soil of weakness.

Techniques for Communicating Adoration and Friendship: Love is a language verbally expressed in bunch ways, and inside the holy obligation of marriage, the craft of articulation becomes fundamental. In this section, we dive into useful systems for sustaining close to home closeness through the statement of adoration and warmth. From ardent encouraging statements to delicate tokens of graciousness, we investigate the assorted manners by which accomplices can convey their adoration and dedication. By dominating the language of adoration, couples make an ensemble of association that reverberates profoundly inside the heart, cultivating a feeling of closeness and having a place. As we uncover the horde ways of communicating love, let us embrace the magnificence of every one of a kind articulation, winding around an embroidery of friendship that ties us together in a tough power of profound devotion.

Making Customs of Association: In the clamoring woven artwork of day to day existence, it's not difficult to neglect to focus on the sacrosanct minutes that tight spot us together as accomplices. In this section, we investigate the significant meaning of making customs of association inside marriage. These customs, whether little and straightforward or stupendous and elaborate, act as anchors that ground us in the ocean of vulnerability, cultivating a feeling of having a place and solidarity. From wake-up routines like sharing some espresso to night customs, for example, ardent discussions before bed, we praise the force of these minutes to reinforce the close to home connections between accomplices. By purposefully cutting out time for association in the midst of the hecticness of life, couples develop a profound feeling of closeness and closeness that supports them through the difficulties and delights of marriage. As we leave on the excursion of making ceremonies of association, let us appreciate the consecrated minutes that help us to remember the significant love that joins us, lighting the blazes of enthusiasm and dedication inside our souls.

Chapter 5: Resolving Conflicts with Grace

Grasping the Idea of Struggles in Marriage: Inside the complicated dance of marriage, clashes frequently arise as regular articulations of the unpredictable elements between accomplices. In this section, we leave on an excursion of investigation into the nuanced idea of contentions inside the hallowed association. We dig profound into the foundations of conflict, revealing insight into the heap sources that lead to conflicts, according to varying points of view and correspondence styles to neglected requirements and assumptions. By looking underneath the outer layer of contention, we reveal unexpected, yet invaluable treasures of knowledge and understanding, perceiving these snapshots of pressure as any open doors for development and more profound association. As we explore the maze of conjugal struggle, let us embrace the insight that exists in these difficulties, manufacturing a way towards more noteworthy concordance and closeness inside our relationship.

Procedures for Solid Compromise: In the pot of marriage, clashes are not enemies to be dreaded yet rather open doors for development and understanding. In this section, we reveal a collection of procedures and methodologies intended to explore clashes with elegance and shrewdness. From undivided attention and sympathetic correspondence to the craft of give and take and discussion, we furnish couples with the apparatuses expected to change conflict into agreement. By developing a feeling of receptiveness and receptivity, accomplices figure out how to move toward clashes with interest as opposed to protectiveness, encouraging a climate where common getting it and goal can thrive. As we embrace the craft of solid compromise, let us introduce another time of organization characterized by sympathy, joint effort, and getting through affection.

Developing Sympathy and Empathy During Conflicts: In the midst of the tumult of conflict, compassion and empathy act as directing lights that enlighten the way towards goal and compromise. In this section, we dig into the extraordinary force of sympathy, welcoming accomplices to step into one another's perspective and view clashes from the perspective of understanding and empathy. By encouraging a profound feeling of sympathy, couples develop a more noteworthy appreciation for one another's points of view and encounters, making ready for shared regard and approval. Through demonstrations of sympathy and thoughtfulness, accomplices figure out how to explore conflicts with beauty and modesty, protecting close to home association and closeness even despite struggle. As we embrace the act of developing sympathy and empathy, let us encourage a feeling of solidarity and understanding that rises above contrasts and fortifies the powers of profound devotion inside our marriage.

Reinforcing the Conjugal Bond Through Valuable Peace promotion: Inside the recurring pattern of conjugal contentions lies a chance for significant development and fortifying of the conjugal bond. In this significant section, we enlighten the extraordinary capability of productive refereeing in sustaining the groundwork of association. By moving toward clashes with modesty and a common obligation to goal, couples encourage versatility and develop closeness. Through productive exchange and common regard, accomplices figure out how to explore conflicts with effortlessness, arising more grounded and more associated on the opposite side. As we embrace the excursion of productive peace promotion, let us outfit the force of difficulty to fashion a bond that endures the everyday hardships, securing our association in affection, understanding, and relentless help.

Chapter 6: Keeping the Flames Alive: Romance and Passion

Significance of Supporting Sentiment: Inside the holy safe-haven of marriage, sentiment fills in as the soul that implants the association with imperativeness and energy. In this section, we enlighten the significant meaning of focusing on sentiment and enthusiasm as fundamental components in supporting the profound association and closeness between accomplices. Through the delicate tokens of friendship, the murmured encouraging statements, and the common snapshots of giggling and happiness, couples feed the flares of want that consume brilliantly inside their souls. By perceiving and regarding the significance of sentiment, couples make a safe-haven of adoration where closeness prospers, and the obligations of fondness extend. As we set out on this excursion of rediscovering the enchantment of sentiment, let us value each valuable second as a chance to light the flash of energy and keep the flares of affection burning inside our marriage.

Imaginative Ways Of reigniting the Flash: In the always advancing scene of marriage, implanting innovativeness and advancement into the texture of sentiment and passion is fundamental. In this part, we set out on an excursion of investigation, uncovering creative procedures and inventive thoughts for renewing the flares of adoration inside the relationship. From unconstrained motions that light the heart to carefully arranged heartfelt trips that encourage the soul, we dive into a mother lode of opportunities for reigniting the flash of energy. Whether it's amazing your cooperate with a sincere love letter, coordinating a candle-lit supper under the stars, or setting out on an experience together, we commend the heap manners by which couples can imbue sentiment and fervor into their daily existences. As we embrace the vast capability of imagination in sentiment, let us revive our connections, changing normal minutes into uncommon recollections that support the spirit and light the blazes of adoration.

Conquering Snags to Closeness: In spite of the profundity of adoration divided among accomplices, deterrents to closeness and energy might emerge inside the marriage. In this section, we go up against these obstructions with fortitude and empathy, looking to comprehend and defeat them together. From the tensions of work and family obligations to the difficulties of stress and exhaustion, we recognize the bunch factors that can hose the blazes of want. Through transparent correspondence, we explore these snags with effortlessness, looking to figure out some mutual interest and arrangements that sustain the closeness between us. With compassion and understanding, we investigate the profundities of our souls, recovering the energy and association that lie torpid inside. As we face these deterrents to closeness, let us arise more grounded and more joined together, producing a way towards more profound closeness and getting through adoration inside our marriage.

Developing a Culture of Appreciation and Sentiment: In the buzzing about of day to day existence, it is not entirely obvious the significance of sustaining a culture of appreciation and sentiment inside the marriage. In this part, we focus a light on the groundbreaking force of little signals and sincere articulations of affection. From a basic "much obliged" for an unparalleled piece of handiwork to an unconstrained hug that conveys the profundity of our fondness, we commend the horde manners by which couples can develop sentiment in their regular day to day existences. By cultivating a climate of appreciation and delicacy, we make a safe-haven of adoration where closeness flourishes and the flares of energy consume brilliantly. As we embrace the act of appreciation and sentiment, let us value every second as a chance to develop our association and fortify the powers of profound devotion that join us in marriage.

7

Chapter 7: Balancing Roles and Responsibilities

Investigating Orientation Jobs and Assumptions: Inside the complex embroidery of marriage, cultural standards and social assumptions frequently shape the division of jobs and obligations between accomplices. In this section, we leave on an excursion of investigation, digging into the nuanced elements of orientation jobs and assumptions inside the setting of marriage. We explore the perplexing transaction of custom and innovation, inspecting how instilled convictions and cultural tensions impact our impression of orientation and the jobs we are supposed to satisfy. By focusing a light on these hidden suspicions and assumptions, we make space for thoughtfulness and exchange, enabling couples to challenge and rethink conventional orientation jobs inside their relationship. As we explore the scene of orientation jobs and assumptions, let us embrace the valuable chance to develop an organization in view of common regard, understanding, and uniformity, where the special qualities and gifts of each accomplice are respected and celebrated.

Techniques for Accomplishing Equilibrium and Equity: In the many-sided dance of marriage, accomplishing an amicable harmony between jobs and obligations requires purposefulness and coordinated effort. In this section, we uncover a collection of down to earth systems and approaches intended to explore the division of work inside the organization. From evenhanded conveyance of family tasks to shared dynamic in monetary issues, we investigate strategies for cultivating a feeling of equilibrium and fairness between accomplices. By cultivating open correspondence and a feeling of participation, couples can co-operate to make a powerful organization where the two people feel esteemed and regarded. As we embrace the excursion of accomplishing equilibrium and correspondence, let us develop a relationship grounded in decency and shared help, where the commitments of each accomplice are perceived and celebrated.

Viable Correspondence and Exchange: At the core of accomplishing amicability in the division of jobs and obligations lies the foundation of powerful correspondence and discussion. In this section, we dive into the extraordinary force of transparent discourse for of exploring the intricacies of organization. By making a place of refuge for articulation and tuning in, couples can participate in helpful discussions about their separate jobs and obligations. Through undivided attention, sympathy, and split the difference, accomplices can figure out something worth agreeing on and foster commonly good arrangements. As we embrace the act of powerful correspondence and discussion, let us cultivate a culture of joint effort and understanding, where contrasts are regarded, and choices are made with common regard and thought.

Establishing a Strong Climate for Self-improvement: Inside the system of marriage, developing a climate that supports the self-improvement and satisfaction of the two partners is fundamental. In this finishing up part, we underline the meaning of making a strong air where people are engaged to seek after their interests and yearnings. By adjusting jobs and obligations to individual qualities and interests, couples can cultivate a feeling of satisfaction and reason inside the rela-tionship. Through consolation and backing, accomplices can set out on an excursion of self-revelation and development, enhancing the organi-zation with their exceptional commitments. As we focus on establishing a strong climate for self-awareness, let us praise the independence and capability of each accomplice, cultivating a relationship that flourishes with shared regard, understanding, and consolation.

Chapter 8: Weathering the Storms Together

Perceiving the Difficulties of Marriage: Inside the holiness of marriage, there exist inescapable difficulties — storms that test the actual texture of our association. In this essential section, we stand up to these difficulties head-on, recognizing their presence and figuring out their possible effect on the relationship. From the preliminaries of monetary strain to the kinds of being a parent, we dive into the horde hindrances that couples might experience along their excursion. By focusing a light on these difficulties, we make space for reflection and exchange, encouraging a more profound comprehension of the intricacies inborn in the conjugal bond. As we explore the rough oceans of marriage, let us defy these difficulties with fortitude and flexibility, manufacturing a way towards more prominent solidarity and strength notwithstanding difficulty.

Developing Versatility and Fortitude: In the pot of misfortune, couples have the chance to produce flexibility and strength that can face any hardship. In this section, we dig into the groundbreaking force of building flexibility as a team, furnishing accomplices with the devices and procedures expected to explore through life's hardships. From developing a mentality of energy and persistence to creating sound survival techniques and critical thinking abilities, we investigate systems for invigorating the connection between accomplices. By embracing difficulties as any open doors for development and learning, couples arise more grounded and more joined together, prepared to confront anything snags might come their direction. As we leave on this excursion of developing versatility and fortitude, let us draw upon the profound well of affection and responsibility that ties us together, rising up out of the cauldron of misfortune more grounded and stronger than any time in recent memory.

Looking for Help and Direction: In the midst of the tempests of life, looking for help and direction can act as an encouraging sign and strength for couples exploring through troublesome times. In this section, we underline the significance of connecting with confided in hotspots for help and advice. Whether it be through proficient treatment, mentorship from experienced couples, or encouraging groups of people inside the local area, looking for help can give important knowledge and point of view. By freeing ourselves up to direction and shrewdness from others, we gain new instruments and procedures for defeating difficulties and reinforcing our relationship. As we rest on the help of others, let us recollect that we don't face the hardships alone, yet rather as a unified front, strengthened by the affection and backing of people around us.

Embracing Development and Change: Inside the pot of difficulty, couples have the amazing chance to embrace development and change that can extend their bond and carry new essentialness to their relationship. In this finishing up section, we praise the versatility and strength fashioned through enduring tempests together. By going up against difficulties head-on and exploring through them with solidarity and determination, couples arise changed, their affection tempered and refined by the preliminaries they have confronted. As we consider the excursion of enduring tempests together, let us embrace the development that has risen up out of difficulty, remembering it as a demonstration of the persevering through force of adoration and responsibility. With hearts sustained by shared insight and brains enhanced by newly discovered shrewdness, let us set out on the following part of our excursion with recharged trust, strength, and love.

Chapter 9: Cultivating Gratitude and Appreciation

The Force of Appreciation: Investigating the groundbreaking effect of appreciation on conjugal bliss and prosperity, perceiving its capacity to encourage appreciation and extend the connection between accomplices.

Rehearsing Everyday Appreciation: Presenting viable methods and ceremonies for integrating appreciation into day to day existence, from saving appreciation diaries to communicating appreciation for one another's activities and characteristics.

Supporting Appreciation in the Relationship: Featuring the significance of sustaining appreciation inside the relationship, encouraging a culture of appreciation and affirmation for one another's commitments and characteristics.

Embracing the Wealth of Affection: Underlining the overflow of affection and gifts inside the marriage, and empowering couples to develop a mentality of overflow and appreciation in their organization.

The Force of Appreciation: Inside the holy obligation of marriage lies a significant yet frequently ignored treasure: the groundbreaking force of appreciation. In this section, we leave on an excursion to investigate the profundities of this powerful power and its capacity to enhance conjugal bliss and prosperity. Appreciation fills in as a brilliant reference point, enlightening the way towards more profound appreciation and association between accomplices. By developing an act of appreciation, couples open the way to an abundance of endowments, both huge and little, that enhance their common process. From the delicate stroke of a caring touch to the murmured expressions of appreciation, appreciation injects each second with a feeling of overflow and wealth. As we dig into the significant effect of appreciation, let us hold nothing back from the gifts that encompass us, developing a feeling of gratefulness that sustains the spirit and extends the power of profound devotion inside our marriage.

Rehearsing Everyday Appreciation: In the hurrying around of day to day existence, ignoring the little marvels and gifts that elegance our path is simple. In this part, we reveal the groundbreaking capability of integrating appreciation into our everyday daily schedule. Through straightforward yet strong practices, for example, keeping an appreciation diary or sharing sincere articulations of appreciation, couples can develop a more profound familiarity with the overflow that encompasses them. By intentionally recognizing and enjoying snapshots of appreciation every day, accomplices develop an outlook of energy and overflow that pervades each part of their relationship. As we embrace the act of day to day appreciation, let us stir to the magnificence and extravagance of the current second, developing a feeling of bliss and satisfaction that supports our hearts and fortifies our bond.

Sustaining Appreciation in the Relationship: Inside the rich soil of marriage, appreciation blossoms as a fragrant bloom, fed by the delicate consideration of accomplices who perceive and respect each other's commitments. In this section, we dive into the significance of supporting appreciation inside the relationship, developing a culture of appreciation and affirmation for the characteristics and endeavors of our cherished. Through thoughtful gestures, encouraging statements, and tokens of appreciation, couples make an environment of warmth and acknowledgment where love can prosper. By putting forth a cognizant attempt to offer thanks for each other's presence, assets, and endeavors, accomplices develop their association and encourage a feeling of shared regard and profound respect. As we sustain appreciation inside our relationship, let us commend the novel characteristics and commitments of our accomplice, winding around an embroidery of adoration that is rich with appreciation and delicacy.

Embracing the Overflow of Adoration: In the depository of marriage, love streams richly, a consistently present stream that feeds and supports the association. In this last section, we welcome couples to embrace the overflow of affection that encompasses them and develop a mentality of appreciation and appreciation. By perceiving the lavishness of affection in the entirety of its structures - from the delicate bit of a hand to the common giggling of a loved second - accomplices hold nothing back from the unlimited gifts that elegance their association. Through appreciation, couples enhance the force of affection, injecting each cooperation with warmth, consideration, and happiness. As we luxuriate in the sparkle of affection's overflow, let us treasure each valuable second, developing a feeling of appreciation that extends our association and enhances our coexistences.

10

Chapter 10: Renewing Vows: Embracing Growth and Change

Pondering the Excursion: As we stand at the limit of recharging, it is fundamental for stop and consider the excursion that has carried us to this second. In this part, we leave on an excursion of reflection, following the way of our marriage from its beginning to the current day. We recognize the exciting bends in the road, the victories and difficulties that have formed our association and shaped us into the people we are today. Through reflection, we gain understanding into the development and changes experienced by the two accomplices over the long run, extending our appreciation for the common history that ties us together. As we think about the excursion of our marriage, let us honor the examples took in, the recollections shared, and the adoration that has supported us through everything, establishing the groundwork for reestablishment and development in the parts on the way.

Reaffirming Responsibility: In the embroidery of marriage, reestablishment offers a sacrosanct chance to reaffirm our obligation to each other. In this section, we embrace this second with veneration, recognizing the difficulties confronted and the adoration that perseveres through everything. Through ardent commitments and commitments, we proclaim our enduring devotion to the association, promising to remain by one another's side through the preliminaries and wins of life.

By reaffirming our responsibility, we honor the sacrosanct bond that joins us, fortifying our purpose to sustain and treasure the adoration that ties us together. As we stand together at this time of restoration, let us draw strength from the profundity of our responsibility, embracing the excursion ahead with fortitude, flexibility, and unflinching dedication.

Embracing Development and Change: Inside the steadily advancing scene of marriage, development and change are unavoidable buddies on the excursion of life. In this part, we embrace the groundbreaking force of development and change, remembering them as normal and vital parts of our common way. We defy the difficulties and advances that go with development with boldness and versatility, exploring them along with beauty and understanding. By embracing change as a chance for individual and social development, we reinforce the groundwork of our organization, extending our association and shared regard. As we leave on this excursion of reestablishment, let us embrace the unavoidable trends with open hearts and receptive outlooks, confiding in the strength of our adoration to bring us through anything that might come our direction.

Praising the Future Together: As we stand on the limit of recharging, we look forward with trust and expectation, commending the unfathomable potential outcomes that lie ahead for our organization. In this last section, we embrace the future with satisfaction and energy, throwing away feelings of trepidation and questions to invite the experience that is standing by. With hearts loaded up with adoration and appreciation, we imagine the fantasies and goals that we share, resolving to walk inseparably into the splendid skyline of tomorrow. Together, we commend the excursion that has carried us to this second, and we look forward with hopefulness, realizing that our adoration will direct us through whatever difficulties and delights might come our direction. As we set out on this new section of our lives, let us embrace the future together, joined in affection, trust, and the faithful obligation to building a daily existence overflowing with joy, development, and satisfaction.

Chapter 11: Conclusion

Thinking about the Excursion: As we come to the zenith of our investigation into the profundities of marriage, it is fundamental for stop and ponder the groundbreaking excursion we have left upon. In this last section, we pause for a minute to glance back at the way we have crossed, recognizing the bits of knowledge acquired and the development experienced en route. From the perspective of thoughtfulness, we return to the examples learned and the insight bestowed, perceiving their significant effect on how we might interpret marriage and connections. By thinking about the excursion, we honor the obligation to individual and social development, commending the achievements accomplished and the difficulties survive. As we stand on the edge of end, let us value the excursion that has brought us here, and convey forward the examples advanced as reference points of direction in our proceeded with quest for adoration, association, and satisfaction inside marriage.

Embracing the Examples Learned: In the embroidery of marriage, each experience is a chance for development and learning. In this finishing up section, we embrace the insight and bits of knowledge gathered from our investigation of the horde aspects of conjugal connections. We perceive the worth of the illustrations learned — the snapshots of win and the difficulties confronted — as impetuses for individual and social change. By embracing the illustrations learned, we enable ourselves to explore the intricacies of marriage with shrewdness and effortlessness, encouraging further comprehension and association with our accomplices. As we convey forward the bits of knowledge acquired, let us honor the excursion of revelation and development, meshing the strings of insight into the texture of our common lives, improving our relationship with profundity, strength, and persevering through adoration.

Resolving to Proceeded with Development: As we bid goodbye to the pages of this book, we stand at the limit of another part in our conjugal excursion — one portrayed by proceeded with development and advancement. In this finishing up section, we concede to the quest for long lasting learning and advancement inside the setting of marriage. We perceive that development isn't an objective yet rather an excursion — a continuous course of self-disclosure, investigation, and refinement. By resolving to proceeded with development, both separately and as a few, we sustain the seeds of probability and likely inside our relationship, encouraging a dynamic and steadily developing organization. As we set out on this excursion of development together, let us embrace the difficulties and open doors that lie ahead with fortitude, strength, and an enduring obligation to the continuous development of affection, association, and satisfaction inside our marriage.

Looking Forward with Trust: As we turn the last pages of this book, we do as such with hearts loaded up with expectation and positive thinking for what's in store. In this closing section, we cast our look forward, embracing the vast potential outcomes that lie ahead for our organization. We confide in the force of adoration and obligation to direct us through the unavoidable highs and lows of marriage, sure about our capacity to endure any hardship that might come our direction. With trust as our compass and love as our directing light, we set out on the excursion ahead with recharged life and excitement. As we step into the obscure, let us truly do so connected at the hip, joined in our common vision of a future overflowing with delight, development, and satisfaction. Together, we embrace the experience that anticipates, knowing that with affection as our anchor, the potential outcomes are boundless.

www.ingramcontent.com/pod-product-compliance
Lightning Source LLC
Chambersburg PA
CBHW021405160726
47994CB00007B/3088